A to Z
of
Corporate
Success Secrets
in
20 Quick Mantras

Pallav Sinha

Illustrations by
Abhinav Sengar and Astitvika Swarnkar

INDIA · SINGAPORE · MALAYSIA

Foreword

Peeling back the layers from an ostensibly dry subject of business and corporate life is no facile endeavor. Yet, Pallav Sinha's invigorating compilation of twenty topics in his book *A to Z of Corporate Success Secrets in 20 Quick Mantras* accomplishes precisely this with aplomb. From the hallowed confines of the boardroom to the cutting-edge of Artificial Intelligence, from the essentials of management to the dichotomy of heroes and scamsters, this book reveals the dilemmas and ironies of the world of business.

Presented in the form of satirical verse, this book is a veritable lexicon of management terms and jargon, which simultaneously focuses a lens on perpetual conflict between antithetical forces: good and evil, long-term and short-term, profit and community, competition and cooperation, risk and brazenness – forces that one encounters on a quotidian basis in the corporate arena. Through his deft interplay of wit and humor, Pallav Sinha reveals that the tug-of-war between these forces finds its resolution not in simplistic binaries, but by allowing a dynamic interplay leading to a natural equilibrium.

Whether you are a seasoned corporate insider or a curious outsider, this light-hearted but incisive work entertains and enlightens. I hope this satire will encourage readers to adopt a fresh perspective on the arcane art of achieving success in the business world.

Shashi Tharoor

New Delhi

Introduction

Does a book as concise as this one really need an introduction? And to which eclectic genre might it belong? Is it a corporate satire, a corporate self-help aspirer, or a breezy stroll through the corridors of business, offering not just comic relief but also a moment for reflection?

The corporate world stands at the forefront of value creation and is one of the most dynamic and prolific institutions ever envisioned by humans. Like all things vibrant and complex, this world and its denizens sport a remarkable array of quirks and idiosyncrasies. This book is your invitation to laugh and ponder as you unveil the opposing forces at play, the dilemmas that professionals regularly contend with, and the art of business beyond mere balance sheets and tangible assets.

Is it the world of the CXO that fascinates you? Are you gripped by the power and delusion of technology and data, or perhaps the innovator's dilemma? Whether it's boardrooms, leadership challenges, management models, risk management, brands, appraisals, corporate success, or IPOs that catch your interest, you'll find it all here in *A to Z of Corporate Success in 20 Quick Mantras*. It's time to B the change you want to C!

Let's get the ball rolling…

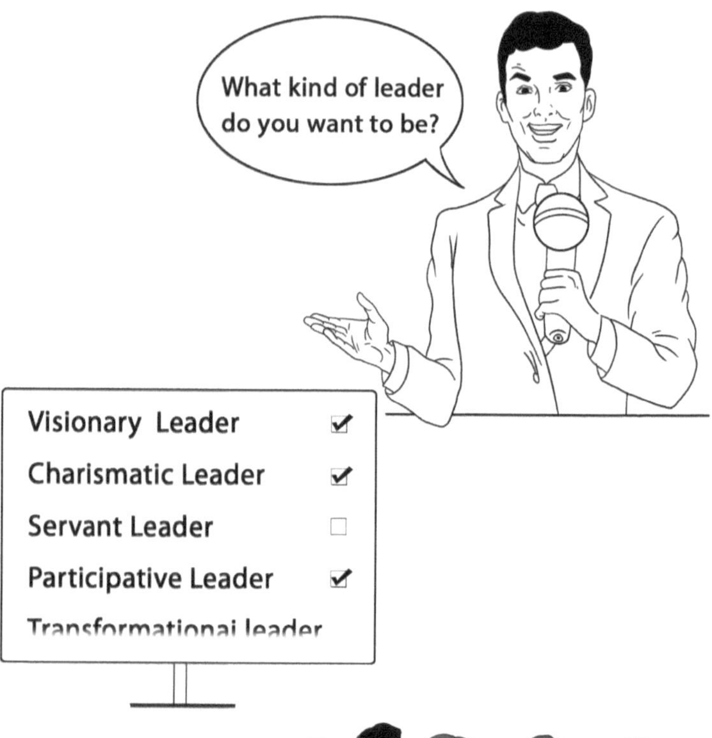

A Leader Be

I'll teach you the ABC[1],   (A)

So you can a leader be   (B)

Diligently follow each cue,   (C)

To ensure you get your CXO due.   (D)

Him or her, they all will err,   (E)

Step by step, you'll get further.   (F)

Soon, it will be within grasp,   (G)

Battle won, more than half.   (H)

Toil, sweat, and industry,   (I)

No plan will be in jeopardy.   (J)

Flying higher than a kite,   (K)

Moving steadily to the light.   (L)

Let me unravel all that's meritorious,   (M)

Of corporate life, quite nefarious.   (N)

Feel the power of oligopoly,   (O)

The art of doing, not philosophy.   (P)

---

[1] Aspire, Believe and Conform

Soon, you'll be at the top of the queue,   (Q)

Non-leaders will need rescue.   (R)

Your promotion's now set in stone,   (S)

Who said it's all about the testosterone?   (T)

Much as you try to unify,   (U)

Plotters, they will vilify.   (V)

Stir you up like wasabi,   (W)

Charge you up like Chairman Xi.   (X)

And that gets us to why and zee,   (Y & Z)

A leader you can surely be:

That we can stamp and now decree.

Your notes ♪♫♪♩♪♫♪♩♪♫♪♩

Commit yourself to success, and it will find you…

Success

Does it come from innovation?

Tinkering outside the box,

And what exactly is the connotation,

Of wearing red and yellow socks?

Add one more feature

And make the customer gasp,

Or make failure your teacher

And strip it down to brass tacks.

Less is more. More or less...

New, improved, and peerless,

The art of hype in progress,

For nothing succeeds like excess.

Does it come from analytics?

Data's the new oil, they say,

Insights - the new business elastics,

Unmatched leverage – that's not hearsay.

Does it come from technology?

The engine under the hood,

Coding, programming, and numeracy,

Though not that widely understood.

Bank from home, or buy on the phone,

Attend the meeting while all alone,

Mine for coins[2] without lifting a stone,

Be TikTok's influencer on the digital throne.

Test, automate, and scale with ease,

APIs make plug-and-play a breeze,

Fail fast[3], but build to last[4],

Cutting-edge of digital tech.

Does it come from employees?

Or was that just a fad,

Relics of the times of your dad?

Would you rather just have talent...

Unleashed and sprinting free,

Or make them go through loops and hoops,

In the jungle of your business zoo?

---

[2]   Cryptocurrency mining

[3]   Fail fast - business philosophy borrowed from Agile software development.

[4]   Build to Last - book by Jim Collins and Jerry Porras, considered to be one of the most influential business books.

Does it come from money?
Magic of financial engineering,
Keeps the beast fed and running,
Investors, vendors, and creditors - dance,
Where cash is king and debt still stings,
Net worth whispers, and monetization wins.

Staying solvent till the end, from the start,
Margins, EBITDA, and Balanced Scorecard[5],
Capital allocation and such arcane arts,
Valuation by the sum-of-parts[6]:
Skills which make this complex craft.

Does it come from model risk and governance?
Diligently following covenants,
In a symphony of compliances, ticking boxes –
Not the fare for cunning foxes.

A tangled web where right and wrong,
Are shades of gray –

---

[5] Balanced Score Card (BSC) was developed by Kaplan and Norton to
     measure performance more holistically.
[6] Sum-of-the-parts (SOTP) valuation calculates total enterprise value
     by separately estimating value of different businesses.

And while it's said that good guys come last,
Is it possible that good companies surpass?

And success, the elusive Houdini,
Will one day target you and me!

Your notes 

3

You will get there when you discover
the joy of missing out (JOMO)…

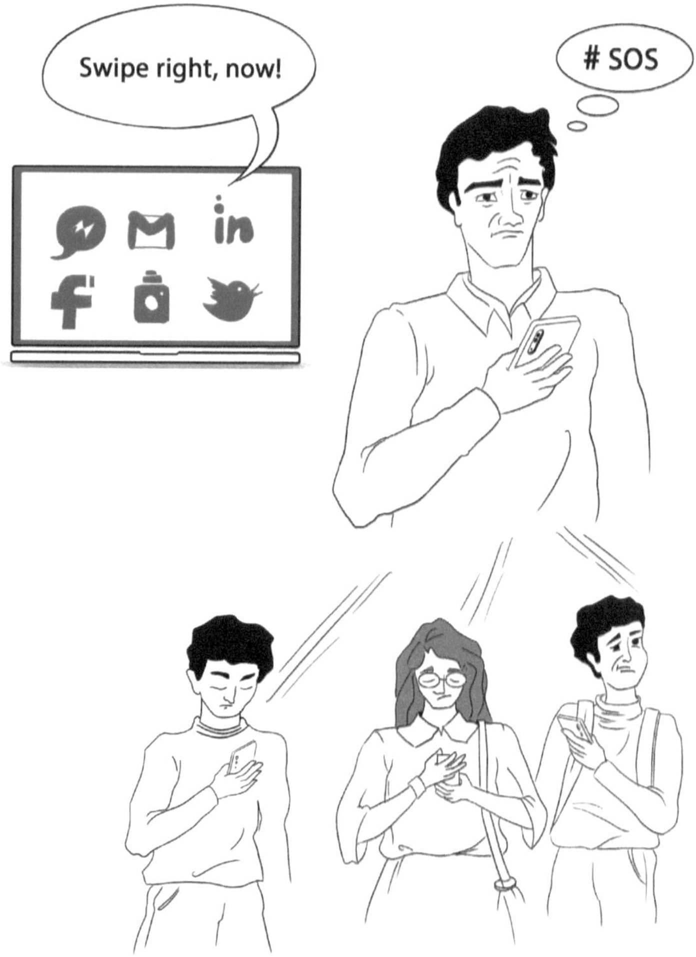

Social Media Salvation

> **Corporate Work Hypothesis for the SMAC world:**
> (Social Mobile Analytics Cloud)
>
> **10:90:1**
>
> 10% of the people ...
>
> Who account for 90% of social media posts ...
>
> Can take credit for no more than 1% of the work done!

Peppy slogans and poor analogies

Of sports, wars, travails, and adversities,

Just the antidote for a soul crushed,

Rousing remedies of a generation rushed:

Seeking salvation on LinkedIn.

Exponentially increasing supply of wisdom,

Matched by demand, equally ravenous,

Soon, making way for the next trite and random -

Nugget from craniums loud and vacuous,

In the echo chamber of empty buzzwords.

Your epiphanies, your alchemy,

Will be pretty crummy,

When you revisit them tomorrow,

Creator and consumer spared much sorrow.

Hold your inspirations,

From being such public revelations –

Biometric markers,

Of social media starkers.

Videos, blogs, and podcasts,

Aspiring gurus of media social,

Bartering wisdom for likes and clicks,

Bludgeoning minds with posts and hacks.

More coaches, fewer players,

Readying us now - layer upon layer,

Shallow foundation and grand edifice,

Upside-down icebergs keeping us transfixed,

Grand pronouncements best nixed.

Creeping feeling of horripilation,

How did we end up –

Loving such an abomination?

Beyond embellishment,

Below the gloss,

Metaverse's gain is life's loss.

Yes – you'll be happier just tweeting,

So much easier to troll and boast,

Repurposing someone's best quote,

For my shiny little LinkedIn post.

Corporate conundrums,

Even daily humdrum,

Hapless magnets for 'wisdom' distilled,

Circling and flashing digital blings.

Pleading for more -- than 280 characters glib,

Or a fancy timeline crafted slick.

A dystopian sequence of juicy click baits,

Will this spate, now, ever abate?

Cowering in fear of the SMAC spate,

To the joy of missing out, we relate!

In the end – there's hope still,

That our digital narrative,

Can be additive, and not net reductive.

4

Known Unknowns

If wisdom's path you fail to trace,

A tangled mess you'll have to face.

Wisdom whispered, knowledge veiled,

In a VUCA[7] world, your senses assailed.

And that is when you hear it said:

"Things that you were never meant to know,

Are worth twice as much, blow for blow."

Thinking beyond the box –

When vision soars till the shoe drops,

Makes you invincible, like the cyborgs,

For cubicle dwellers, a much-needed detox,

The magic key that opens all locks.

I know that business is the Art of War,

But I don't know:

If it's also an Act of Love?

Where Sun Tzu's might,

Meets a gentler light,

---

[7] VUCA – volatile, uncertain, complex, ambiguous

And compelling exhortations,

Of passion and profitable enterprise,

Take on a truer and warmer hue.

I know the aphorism - of the enemy of my enemy,

But I don't know:

If it's far better to opt for friends,

Than to rely on bridges built on fragile trust

Of frenemies and crumbling dust?

I know that teamwork is to acquiesce,

But I don't know:

If it's better to raise my voice,

And just hold my ground?

For minds aligned in harmony,

May spark a splendid symphony,

Or perhaps, just painful ignominy!

I know that it's our nature to conform,

But I don't know:

If it takes outliers, strange and bold,

To make our future bright as gold?

I know that success we must crave,

But I don't know:

If it just does us enslave,

And makes sanity go away?

Do ambition's fires leave us whole,

Or do they burn our eternal soul?

I know that careers are long and rewarding,

But I don't know:

If life may be too short,

To miss the vistas and the songs?

How to make work and life entwine?

That's the secret of all times.

I know that the DEI[8] is cast,

But I don't know:

If it's just in stone,

Or deeply in our hearts?

Will its seeds disperse,

And create a charter for the universe?

I know that we must our planet save,

But, I don't know:

---

[8] DEI: Diversity, equity and inclusion.

If that's best done by decarbonizing,

Or by positively ionizing,

Negativity that humanity is trivializing?

While our blue-green planet is vaporizing!

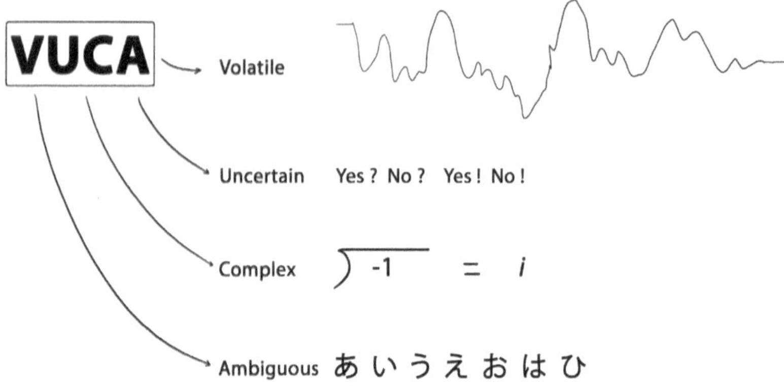

I know that knowledge is power,

But I don't know:

If data, which is the new oil,

Could power my home for an hour?

And I also don't know:

If knowing what we leave unknown,

Is that a splendid superpower?

Your notes ♪♫♪♫♪♫♪♫

Free the
market
Money makes the
world go round

5

Prodigious Profits

It's true what they say -- the bottom line's divine,

For corporations, a sweet, entrapping rhyme,

As long as it compounds and growth abounds,

Future cash flows are worth a pretty pound.

But once, these profits lined the royal purse,

A monarch's treasure; not the market's curse!

Then sailed a buccaneer, seafaring and bold,

The Dutch East India Company, a story to behold.

Its shareholders feasted on spices and gold,

Empires bled dry, being bought and sold!

For its shareholders mattered,

Not the colonies' poor souls.

Four centuries did East India Company reign,

And then some others deciphered the game.

Now giants of a different breed take flight,

Microchip, not gunpowder, their might.

Apple, which blue-eyed techies bite,

Mints money with each click and swipe

... On its oh so beauteous device!

And its NASDAQ cohort, is with acronyms stuck,
MAAMA and FAANG[9], they guzzle every buck.

Oil barons once held sway, like Exxon's might,
Bell Labs the innovations star, that lit up the skies,
Ford and Chrysler, titans of the road,
Now Tesla purrs where ICE engines roared.
Empires that once glowed and then ebbed,
Like GE, a fallen colossus
In Welch's wake, mired in losses.

Pharma giants battle on with R&D and IPR,
Retail wars grapple, with consumers oh so fickle,
Walmart and Amazon, jostle with SKUs and price,
A digital funambulist's dizzying delight.
Nokia, Kodak, Xerox –
Names that in our memories stay,
Even as the companies tatter and fray,
Victims of business and profit charade.

---

[9] FAANG – Facebook; Amazon; Apple; Netflix and Google.
    MAAMA – Meta; Amazon; Apple; Microsoft and Alphabet.

Profit or loss, beyond spreadsheets and gloss,

Grit and valor, cut from a different cloth,

Like the expert navigator of centuries past,

Steering by stars, sextants, and chutzpa,

Business barons bravely forge a glorious path,

Guided by instinct, ambition, and smarts.

Navigating through business cycles, revenue pools,

In a time where software eats the world,

And JAWS[10] of revenue to expense -

Itch to clamp shut, seeking fresh blood.

Business braves armed with management tools,

Juggling daggers of capital,

Majestic and deadly – both at once!

Blending talent, teamwork, and culture,

A most proficient organization structure.

Strategic thinking about industry and trends,

Of customers assets and size of TAM[11],

NPS[12] lifeblood through monetizable strands,

---

¹⁰ JAWS: Is the rate of change of revenue vs. rate of change of expense. A positive JAWS implies revenue is growing faster than expense and margins are improving.

¹¹ TAM: Total addressable market

¹² NPS: Net Promoter Score

Multiple levers in dexterous hands,

Awaiting the corporate jinn's command.

Free markets bare their animal spirits:

'Winner takes all,' and from there emerges,

The hope of electric 'trickle-down' surges:

An illusion and belief,

Of a somewhat level playing field!

Neutron Jack[13] and Friedman, prophets bold,

Of shareholders' primacy - their stories told,

'Profits for owners,' they did sing,

For a rising tide lifts all boats,

Which is why it's Shareholder Capitalism's[14] abode.

Then Kotler raised the customer's plea,

'Focus on the user' was his decree,

And in their delight, there's a profit spree!

[13]   Jack Welch who was Chairman of GE was called Neutron Jack for firing people while leaving buildings intact.

[14]   Shareholder Capitalism was first enunciated by the Economist Milton Friedman. According to this, corporations have one goal - to maximize profits.

Is Stakeholder Capitalism[15] the answer we seek?

Or are CSR and ESG really burdens we bear?

Though for employees and communities –

A breath of fresh air!

Is Polman's[16] Net Positive worth a think,

With profits the foundation of sustainable living?

Activist investors such as Larry Fink[17],

And CEOs of various ilk

Have expressed a commitment,

Deep and abiding,

To keep both their planet and company thriving.

---

[15] Stakeholder Capitalism is the concept endorsed by the CEOs' Business Roundtable which says that the other stakeholders such as communities, employees, environment, regulators are equally important as shareholders and profit maximization is not a company's sole objective.

[16] Paul Polman was the Chairman of Unilever and in his book Net Positive he espoused the concept of a corporation that gives more than it takes, and does no harm.

[17] Larry Fink is the Chairman of BlackRock which is the largest Asset Management company in the world. Asset Managers have become activist investors in companies.

The lesson is this:

Profit is a hammer with which you pass or fail,

Let not corporate exuberance; make the world a nail.

Harmony in business, community, and earth,

Balancing ledgers beyond monetary worth.

Your notes

27

No pain,
no gain

Comfort Zone

I can see from up here
You're running downhill.
It's the easy way that leads nowhere,
Summits beckon...
They can be your perch, still.
Why be a hamster in a maze?
You're the one to trailblaze!

The speed you feel,
Aren't well-oiled wheels,
And every bit of joie de vivre
Will make your soul and body weep,
When you see the place you reach –
It's not the mountain, nor the beach!

But if you stop and turn around,
It may make you lose your bounce
And for a time, you're the clown
Who strains and groans yet makes no ground,
Looking foolish has its gains,
Serpentine path to the gates of fame.
Pain and gain go hand in hand,
Goes the wisdom of a distant land,

Running downhill – we all can!

Time to turn your gaze and embrace,

The uphill slog, not a tick-box paradigm,

Discover purpose – infinitely more divine:

Not moving the needle, one decimal point at a time.

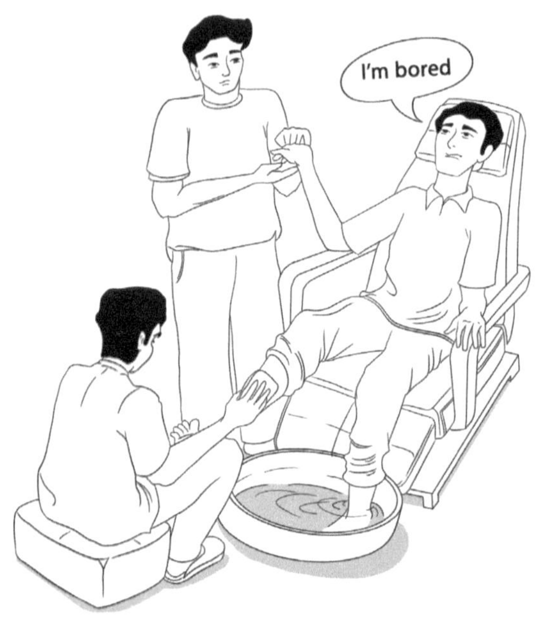

Soon, your quads and glutes will grow,

With wisdom, you will overflow,

It will then be worth the change

Struggling up the mountain range,

As you observe the vistas, broad and grand,

You'll know the climb was worth the calloused hands.

Your notes

Keep   till   music
dancing   the   plays

Dam the Scams

Business makes money,

Attracting swindlers like honey:

Insiders, outsiders, and bestriders,

Gaming the system like joyriders.

Chorus:

Straight and narrow path not taken:

Lust, greed, and sub-prime alchemy[18].

Did it start with South Sea bubblin',

Or new-age Lehman tumbling?

Jeff Skilling's Enron ride was thrilling.

Smart little Liz Holmes a loss

In the resplendent story of Theranos[19],

McKinsey's Rajat[20] was once white as a lily,

But he did trip and look downright silly.

---

[18] Preceding the financial crisis of 2008, sub-prime housing loans were packaged into Mortgage-Backed-Securities (MBS) and given the highest credit ratings reserved for prime loans - alchemy of subprime loans via financial engineering.

[19] Elizabeth Holmes, once a widely acclaimed biotech entrepreneur and founder of Theranos was indicted for fraud.

[20] Rajat Gupta - McKinsey global head and widely respected business advisor who was indicted by the SEC of Insider Trading.

Tally-ho, tally-ho, tally-ho,

Hold your horses, don't just go,

LBOs, CDOs[21], and cryptos,

All of which can stub your toes.

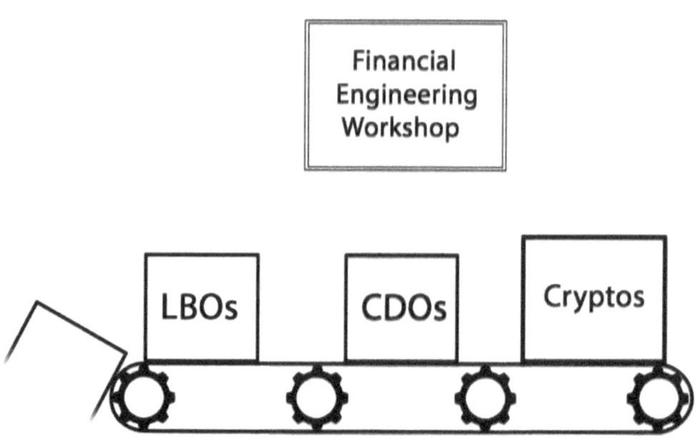

Mumbo jumbo gets the dumbos,

It's a daisy chain of greater fools.

Chuck, the Prince of Citi[22] said:

"Keep dancing till the music ends."

Crypto's stories like FTX,

Inky darkness post special effects.

Governance, regs, and compliance,

Are for those who lack the spine for defiance?

---

[21] Leveraged Buyouts and Collateralized Debt Obligations.

[22] Chuck Prince was the CEO of Citi before the financial crisis. Now remembered for his infamous quote 'you've got to dance till the music plays.'

Epstein, Madoff, and Wirecard's fraud[23] –

Were they ever worth the reward?

Chorus:

Straight and narrow path not taken:

Lust, greed, and sub-prime alchemy.

Did it start with South Sea bubblin'.

Or new-age Lehman tumbling?

Before you ride the tiger,

Or stop being a striver

Remember, it's a sugar rush

Just another kinda drug,

Choose a diet of humble pie,

Which will always keep you dry.

Too Big to Fail

---

23   Jeffrey Epstein, Bernie Madoff and Wirecard are all individuals and
      companies indicted for fraud and running Ponzi schemes.

But if you choose to be a whale,

You're then – 'Too Big to Fail'[24].

Keep dancing till the music plays,

In the hope of sunnier days.

---

[24] Some banks and financial institutions were so large and due to the inter-connectedness of banks and financial companies, they could not be allowed to fail and it was assumed that Central Banks would need to bail them out.

Your notes 

I'm conscience your ol' friend,
I've come to talk to you
again!

8

Conscience Call

When conscience whispers on the line,

Do you pick up or hit decline?

Siren song of the ethics clan,

Oh, such a challenge to withstand!

For your moral compass buried deep

Lulls you to a chloroformed sleep.

Should you wake to move and shake?

Seems like that's a big mistake.

Climb the ladder, corpse by corpse -

Aim for the moon, not treetops!

Atonement awaits, some distant day,

For now, let these mantras light your way:

Double bottom-line[25],

Of profit, and

For the integrity inclined...

Walking the straight and narrow line.

---

[25] Double bottom-line (DBL) refers to an additional bottom-line for firms apart from the conventional measure i.e. profit. The second bottom-line measures social impact that is brought about an enterprise.

Social impact has its takers,

Sustainability its share of fakers,

For those to whom equity means shares, not sharing,

Accumulating a fortune - their only caring.

Diversity, equity, and inclusion (DEI),

Just principles for a moral high?

Capitalism's desperate disparity,

Or a saga of equal hilarity:

Climate actions COPs[26],

And those sleeping on their watch.

Accountability, Responsibility,

Honesty, and Integrity –

Principles for eternity...

Until the rubber and road meet,

And we're on corporate mean street.

For every good business manager

Has gotta be a 24x7 striver,

An obsessive process ascriber,

Then, is there time for ESG[27],

And leaving behind a legacy?

---

[26] COPs - Conference of Parties refers to meeting of governments to
      evaluate progress against climate action goals

[27] ESG: Environment, Social and Governance

Conscience takes a vacation,

Let progress be your guide,

In the corporate jungle,

Must you jettison ethics to survive?

Your notes 

9

Career Conundrums

What's a career and what's a job?
And would you trade your potential
For it all?

Cash cow or future star,
Here and now or further afar?
Greatest boss or boss' pet,
Good with numbers or tales well met?

What you are, is what you get
One should never not forget,
A 'better you' could show up yet.

For the lean, mean, fighting machine,
Career options are umpteen
No feather beds for avatars,
Be yourself – blemishes and scars.

Fresh thinking in vast blue oceans[28],

Nose to grindstone in operations,

Customer-supplier negotiations,

Finance, employees, and their tribulations,

Technology, risk, and other such functions.

Big fish in a small pond, or small in big,

A shark in the tank, and you're lit.

Whatever your failings and your skills,

You've gotta be one step ahead of being bit.

Put a shark in the tank

---

[28] Red and Blue Ocean Strategies refer to the market with the former
being hyper competitive and a zero-sum game for competitors.
Blue Ocean strategies allow for expansion of the market, making
competition irrelevant

Raising a toast to your promotion,

Promoting your work for the raise,

Getting both is cause for elation,

Neither? – it's time to self-appraise!

Deep and somber introspection

Looking back and connecting the dots[29],

Though not quite like Steve Jobs!

---

[29]   In his commencement address at Stanford, Steve Jobs said that one
has to trust one's gut and instinct and the dots will connect in the
future. It was a call for 'following your passion.'

Once you know what matters -

It's the teamwork of solo riders,

A job that doesn't ignite your passion,

Churns talent pools and spikes attrition.

For all your strengths and fatal flaws,

Stay one step ahead, by embracing the cause.

Your notes 

Management alphaβet Soup
·SWOT ·Leverage
·ROCE ·WACC   ·LTV
·CAC   ·(P/B-1)
Repeat after me...

Management 101

ARR[30] you on track,

Or does it feel like a nail rack? (Days crawl; years fly)

Thirsting for the days, somehow

When everything will be just wow! (When you'll hear:
PAT, PAT, PAT)

Aim for the stars, but not those that twinkle,

For here we like to keep things simple,

Take no prisoners, it's the art of war,

Build our EBITDA - or say au revoir. (Earnings or bust, you
see!)

Now for Lesson 1-0-1,

It's time that you be Number One:

Ensuring Return on Capital you employ,

Exceeds Weighted Average Cost to deploy. (ROCE >
WACC)

---

[30]   ARR – annual recurring revenue

Debt to equity?

Price to book?

Palms get sweaty,

Yet, ice-cold look!

Corporate warriors

Are not born, but made, (MBA maketh the man)

No reason then, to be dismayed.

Audit and Risk,

Marketing and Sales,

Treasury and Fitch

Digital fails!

Cybersecurity, let's not forget,

Phishing trips and sunk cost stings:

Reputational loss and such misgivings.

Balance Sheets with Free Cash Flows?

P&Ls with highs and lows?

Derivatives and off-book dealings,

Attract those VCs with no feelings,

Manage well and get that PAT[31],

Strategic Plans with competitor stats.

Human Capital's cold crevice,

------

[31]   PAT – profit after tax

SWOTs and triple-bottom lining[32],

Led by Business Process redesigning.

Internal, external, micro, and macro

Long-term, short-term, strategic and tactico,

Marketing's smoke and mirrors sing,

Success? It's as easy as you think –

Just fake it till the applause rings.

4Ps your compass in the fog, (Marketing-mix)

Brand value - the wherewithal.

Without a moat, it's the open road,

Strategy is all dagger and cloak.

Don't let CACs[33] get out of hand,

LTV[34] must blossom and grow,

Cost-to-Income – keep it low,

Product demand the real boast.

KRAs the metrics that command

What you measure the team delivers,

---

[32] Triple bottom-line: Extends the objectives of a company beyond profits to Planet and People, in pursuit of sustainability
[33] CAC – customer acquisition cost
[34] LTV – lifetime value

And you mustn't brook no delays,

Time is money, and money's divine,

Rewards for others? Give them a sliver! (CTC framework)[35]

It's a world, divided between takers and givers,

By thinkers, doers, and clever deceivers

Choose your side – the team of achievers.

Remember Management 101:

Never let it seem like fun,

Scenario Planning and Value Chains,

Covey's habits and Mintzberg's roles[36],

Keep management models on endless scroll.

---

[35] CTC framework: Is the cost to company, or compensation plan for a firm.

[36] Different management tools e.g. Stephen Covey popularized the habits of effective managers. Similarly, Mintzberg outlined a framework of roles of managers, in which they are required to not only be functional specialists, but also organizational generalists.

Your notes 

(11)

Mixed Reality

The art of the possible, for rats in cubicles,
Where dreams in chrome and glass combust,
Souls shrink, weighted under ambitions robust.
Skyscraper promises and purposeful gleams,
While those beneath, mouth quiet screams.

Janus mask of triumph and tears,
Ecstasy peaks and gnawing fears.
Of career graphs and hagiography—
Passions primed to perpetuity,
And dedication dumped in terminal atrophy!
Learning while forgetting the past,
Making fleeting moments last.

Grand launches, smart and spiffy,
Vanquished by storms of reality gritty.
Buffering impatience, glitchy digitality,
Strategic plans cleaved bare and raw,
Victims of execution, the last straw.

Chasing more cheese, chiming more bells,

Pavlovian puppets, their story it tells,

Moving up Maslow's hierarchy,

In enterprise our trust, not plutocracy.

For business' risk-reward play,

Is the progress engine with power brakes,

Portmanteau of dreams and reality,

Which soothe, yet sting,

In a work-life union, most rewarding!

Your notes

59

Work is for robots.
Leisure for humanity

Autonomous Corporation

Is it time for liberation's rhyme,

For cars and corporates sublime?

Autonomy from human folly's yoke,

From obsessive suits with rising hopes—

Eventually reaching,

Disappointing destinations.

Corporations running on inviolable code,

Lines of logic—cold and bold,

In millions... deterministic and precise...

Algorithmic—

Like a doom-scrolling timeline.

Optimized for profit's embrace,

No duplicitous emotional trace,

Meeting each quarterly forecast,

No exceptions, no laggards!

Blackbox of Deep Learning[37],

Pretty shallow on every yearning.

Computer Vision; Corporate Missions,

Data Science for Luddites,

Smart Contracts[38] forged on silicon sands,

Covenants sans tortuous discussions,

Yielding predictable progression.

Moving forward—no heart, no hands!

---

[37] AI created algorithms and neural networks not fully understood by their creators.

[38] Ethereum blockchain pioneered programs, normally of a contract between two parties.

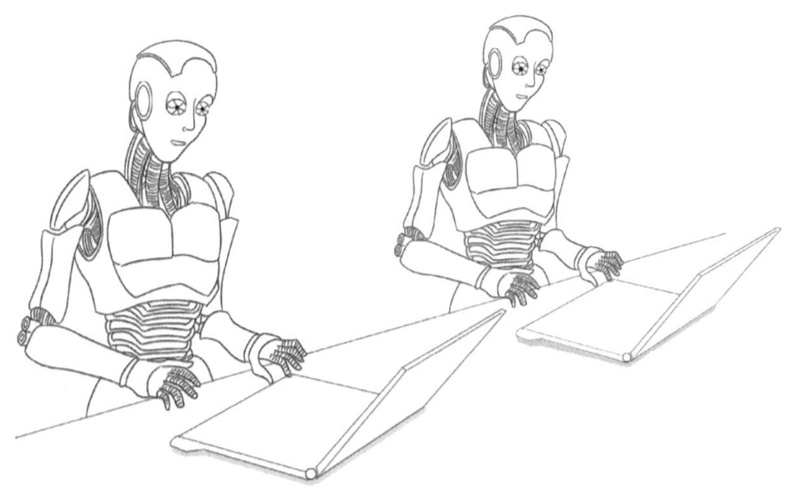

Blockchain and triple entry,

Immutable for years aplenty.

Strategies spun by neural networks,

Surpassing humanity's fading sparks.

Holographic avatars taking the helm,

We're mere shadows in their digital realm.

Seeking sentient singularity[39],

Serendipitously saving humanity?

Robots toiling night and day,

In leisure's gilded cage, we stay.

Yet whispers linger in the code

Of Machine Learning's once human chore,

Leaving us yearning... not for more,

But for that which we cursed before.

---

[39] *In Artificial Intelligence (AI) singularity refers to the point when AI surpasses human intelligence and when computer technology is out of human control.*

Your notes 

65

$$X(f) = \int_{-\infty}^{+\infty} x(t)e^{-j2\pi ft}\, dt$$

Tech Bros

Yes, you know it all,

Especially—equations.

But nothing in life is balanced.

Algorithms' problematic solutions,

Luckily no love bugs in the code,

Or even your DNA.

Ferrari
LV
BBC
PAYPAL
TESLA
NVIDIA
adidas
Gillette
Nestlé
a

Brand Ambassador

What magic is in a brand?
Much beyond a mere stamp!
Top-of-mind unaided recall,
Of Coke, Nestle and Adderall.

You think they're jewels of diamond shine,
Rolex, Dior, Hermes and brands divine.
But Google, Meta and tech,
Offer freebies and reel you in,
Your data is the gold that lights their fire,
A billion likes, a hidden desire.

Walmart's aisles and Apple's golden bite,
Chinese whispers and Alibaba's surprise,
Though Dell, Disney and Deloitte might.
Tata is steeled for Tesla's flight.
Netflix binges and Nike races,
Also-rans fester—in dusty spaces.

Nourish a business
With a healthy brand—
(Which makes us crave a Big Mac,
Add fries while you can!)
That's the secret to understand,
Brand furnace that's forever cranked.

Luxe, quality, trust embodied,
Consistency and innovation go hand-in-hand,
They used to last a few decades and forty...
Now trends shift like desert sands,
Brands life's a flicker, held in AI hands.

In a world that's taken with personal branding,

Endorsements from celebrities upstanding,

In a steeplechase of Deepfake,

Kardashian contours, pixels and pills,

Human obeisance to dopamine thrills.

Toast the branding gods who reign,

Influencers in media, where sanity's insane!

Ponder the power we have handed away,

Question the price we willingly pay.

Your notes

Customer

Shareholder

Employee

Community & Regulator

Appraisals

You think it's time,

For glory and sunshine?

Boss: (Squinting into the phone calendar)

      "Let's meet and dust off your goal sheet!"

Me: "You know I was too busy (*you creep*),

      To transpose those targets,

      From a remote corner of my mind,

      Where light does not shine,

      To digital footprints in the sands of time."

Boss: (Sighs, steepling fingers)

      "Meet me tomorrow, KRAs in hand,

      You ain't finding a kinder boss in Corporate Neverland.

      Professionally, you're in disarray!

      You've heard me say - a little focus,

      Is better than management hocus pocus!"

Me: (Next day: Shuffling papers with a hopeful look)

      "Here it goes:

      In my watch, did business grow,

      Leaps and bounds, it wasn't slow!

      Efficiency in Ops, I have the chops,

Customers loved our features and bugs;

Made teams work, even slugs!"

Boss: (Peering over glasses)

"The numbers don't add,

Costs are up,

Share price tanked,

While attrition's up!"

Me: (Juggling jargon, grasping at straws)

"Capex and investments,

Will pay back soon,

Long-term achievements,

Will trump the short-term swoon!

Market analysts will soon realize,

Competition we are sweeping aside.

Then, for the stock, it's a one-way ride!"

Boss: (Polishing monogrammed cufflinks)

"Your passion should burn...

Show initiative out of turn...

We're a business in a hurry,

Your presence should ease my worry,

It's just my luck, that I'm well and truly curried!"

Me: (Disguising panic with a reassuring look)

"Many train wrecks were headed your way,

My deft ring-fencing made them fade away!

(*Maybe some song and dance and a drama queen,

Would have helped the crisis remain evergreen*)."

Boss: (Animatedly now, sweeping arms expansively)

"More should have been done on ESG,

To consultants, we should have paid less fee,

Our digital transformation is slow,

Competitors are pulling the rug below,

Our debt should have been rated higher,

And our IPO was no flier!"

Me: (Desperate dance of cornered weasel)

"Impossible trinity – I know the easel!

Focus you taught, not random walk,

When firestorms brew and tensions stalk!"

Boss: (Eyes softening, hint of a smirk)

"Chew gum, blow bubbles and walk,

That, my friend, is the CEO's lot!

To be best positioned for my job,

I'll draft you to learn the not-so-facile craft."

Me: (Mixed emotions of hope and despair)

"Multi-tasking? That, sir, is my true calling!

But today, it seems to have rained on my parade!

Though my varied skillset is no charade!"

Boss: (Leaning back, predator with cornered prey)

"Patience and perseverance, infallible tools,

To convert your potential and get you the moon."

Me: (Panic and hopelessness)

"Potential! Growth? Empty chimes!

A stock grant like last time,

Or comp adjustment's shine,

Should rightfully have been mine."

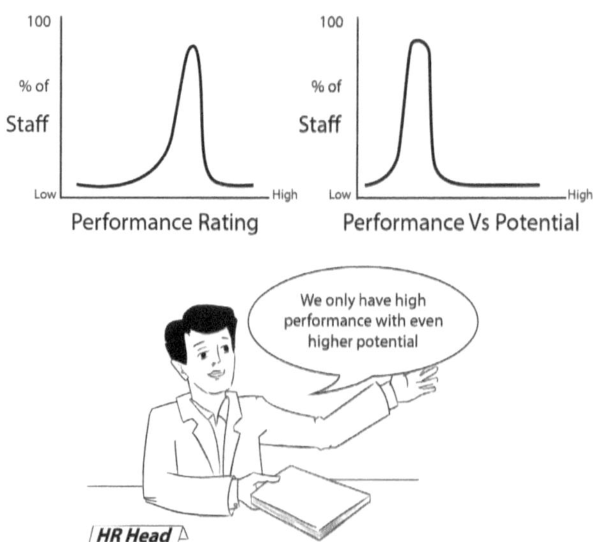

Boss: (Encouraging and enthusiastic)

"You are among our top performers!

(*as are 90% of others, at your level,

Ironically, despite such pervasive glow,

Our company seems stuck so low*).

The best things in life,

Are worth waiting for,

You might have gotten a fright

If it happened outright!

Your comp: both fixed and variable,

Exceed budgets available!

So, let's keep it tight,

Next year I promise a sweet surprise!"

Me: Boss, if you're feeling humped,

And I'm well and truly jumped,

Who is having all the fun?

Your notes

16

Work in progress…

Future of Work

Work from home (WFH) and hybrid work,

Leisure in Office (LIO) for habitual shirks,

Hot desking dramas,

Pajama party at AM nine –

Is fun going to be work again?

Your notes ♪♫♩♬♪♩♫♪♫♩♬

17

Don't let the stars get in your eyes…

Idol No More

You are my inspiration,

Nothing less, and

Definitely nothing more – anymore.

By putting you on a pedestal,

I could look you in the eye.

Now searching for a new idol,

--- high and low.

A new flawed idol.

Your notes

18

Not everyone's espresso…

Start-up Non-starter

Dramatis personae in this start-up kerfuffle:

Spicy Rogan (Spicy) – Founder 1. Seasoned consultant. King of "phone call after six."

Double You Bablu (W Bablu or W) – Founder 2. Corporate misfit and dreamer with a shaky grip on reality.

W Bablu stands among the ruins, ruminating.

Flashback: Hubris and High Hopes

When W and Spicy did decree -

They're now on a start-up spree,

Fueled by ambition's fire,

Soaring skywards, even higher.

Trepidation and excitement ensued,

In the sunrise of hopes and dreams they're imbued,

And suddenly the world is multi-hued.

But in all this glitter,

Did crawl some nasty critters.

W with some taste of corporate wins

Which makes him think he has it within,

To make the switch from suited mediocrity

To the acme of start-up aristocracy.

Spicy - the czar,

Of strategy and schemes bizarre,

Can do it all,

But only from afar.

To the consultant's symphony,

He believes the world must rhapsody.

ACT I:

W and Spicy's start-up raises funds at an attractive valuation (i.e. minimum dilution[40]) and is ready to roll. Yet, bigger dangers lurk when there is joy, exhilaration, and celebration all around.

Spicy: I've done my bit.

The company has funds.

Time for you guys to go great guns.

Now off I go – you lot have fun!

W: (*Thinking to himself*)

Someone feels he's too clever,

But that's the hand which has been dealt.

Let's keep moving in fair weather,

And our boat will be ashore,

With or without Spicy, for sure.

Lesson One: *Businesses built on foundations faulty,*

Will fail despite facades lofty.

All shoulders to the wheel,

That is the start-up deal.

Many tragedies yet befall,

After the funding waterfall.

---

[40] Dilution is the equity stake that a founder gives up, each time she raises funds. Total dilution in equity therefore depends on the amount of funding raised and the valuation ascribed to the company at fund raise.

ACT II

The start-up is operational, and there's a buzz in the air. W and the team are pushing slowly against an invisible weight...

W and his team,

A mountain did they push,

Chasing vanity metrics,

Which for their goal they mistook.

Spicy though, was MIA,

For a mere start-up

Couldn't come in his way.

Spicy: I'm only a phone call away,

    On Fridays after six. ("Thirty after 10 pm your time")

    Let's slot two hours then,

    When every problem I'll nix.

W: Whatever happened to:

    Roll-up your sleeves,

Sweat and bleed,

Why should I be the one

Wrestling with the pigs?

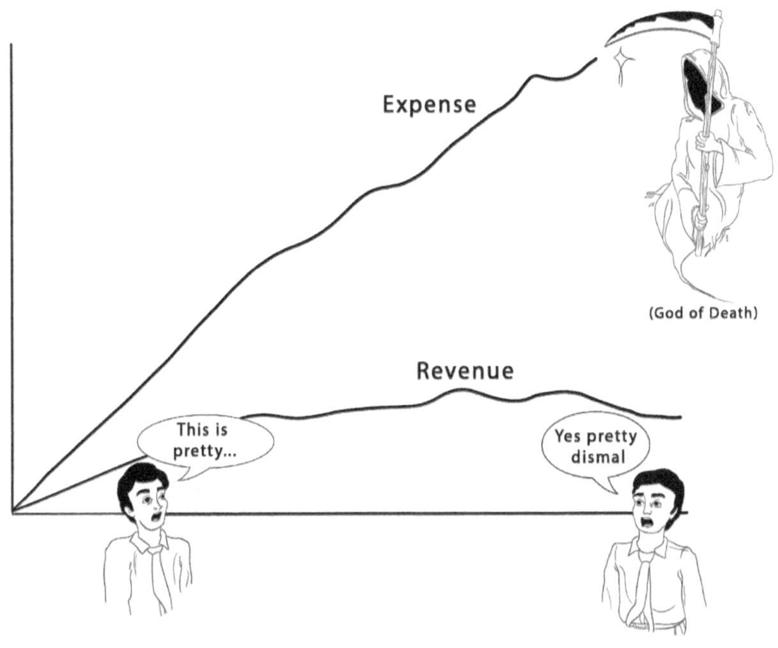

Lesson Two: Business battles are won in the ring.

Puppeteering is not getting you no bling.

Chasm between dreams and deeds,

Vast...and wide,

Bridged only by the grind.

ACT III

Battered by bruising battles,

A funding famine now looming,

W and Spicy, hat in hand,

Face up to the VC clan,

Rolling out the spiel,

Tango of hope and despair.

W: That seemed to go well,

          Touching a tender chord.

Spicy: Last one was also swell,

          In social impact they revel...

          But funding delay will be our death knell.

W: Looks like we'll yet come out upright.

Spicy: I just wish the VCs weren't so uptight,

          This US\$ 1 million ARR ask is asinine.

W: That seems just so out of sight...

Spicy: Positive unit economics!

          Key metric tracking!

          There! You have the mantra!

          'You've gotta fake it till you make it,'

          Rapid scaling is the tantra.

W: We need all hands-on deck,

          Not consultants hanging...

          Like millstones around the neck!

Lesson Three: Heed the MVP's[41] quiet truth,

Shun the swift scale-up ruse,

Burn: less trophy more taboo.

Pivot, pirouette, and then renew.

ACT IV

Failing to secure another round of funding puts the startup under intense pressure.

Funding flops,

Shut startup shops,

Which leaves W and Spicy's venture,

Fighting a losing battle in the bunker.

Spicy: We're in serious trouble,

---

41   Minimum Viable Product

And unless we find a way,

There'll not just be trouble,

It'll burst this bubble!

W: Seems like we've had our last hurray!

I've said it before and say it now,

Revenue model is in disarray.

Our tech and product – sinking dhows.

Spicy: Unit economics is the panacea

Of all the ills – my deah.

Metrics we had to measure

To make this business a treasure.

Lesson Four: Bare essentials,

Where less is more,

Especially when it comes to egos.

Big teams, a distraction

To lead you astray.

Don't get to a point,

Where the solution is to slash,

For by then, the cat's out of the bag.

Product Success,

With sky-high NPS[42].

Value creation,

With customer attestation.

---

[42]   Net Promoter Score

ACT V

All the promises lie undone,

Where there was once effervescence

There's now enervation and ennui.

W: For a brief period, the light shone bright...

Spicy: So many things we didn't do right!

        (Thinking aloud)

        Thankfully my other investments are watertight.

W: Now we have a right royal mess to clear...

Spicy: If only my advice you'd hear.

        (But silence fills the air.)

Lesson Five: A corporate gig and startup are almost like the African elephant and Indian elephant: they look strikingly similar but are genetically very dissimilar.

So much so,

You may not know,

These elephants

Cannot interbreed!

When founders ignore,

The elephant in the room,

You already know the score.

The startup journey, solitary and steep,

A dance with destiny where wounds are deep,

For the brave who snatch the opportunities in time,

Therein, the essence of entrepreneurship thrives.

Start-up palette

Build better Products	
Create better Value	
Implement better Processes	
Target better Opportunities	
Nurture better Teams	
Cultivate better Culture	
Drive better Engagement	
Conceptualize better Strategies	
Attract better Investors	
Handle Risks expertly	
Manage Finances prudently	
Respect Governance standards	
Anticipate Future trends	
Forget past rapidly	

Your notes ♪♫♩♪♫♪♪♫

93

We work in
shadows, but try
not to be shady

Boardroom Brouhaha

If glorious success for Boards is the ask,

That's an oxymoron, and a Sisyphean task!

For a Board is feted, if at all,

When nothing of note is recalled,

As its tenure does placidly pass.

Working in the shadows,

Reigning for nothing, but fame,

(Though that's totally deranged!)

Steadying the ship by being the ballast,

No crisis rocks the ship they hold,

Itself proffering a muted palette,

While the company and management's

Deeds do sparkle and shine:

Survive, not thrive - the board's decree.

Yet stories they abound,

Of directors running their ships aground:

When Yahoo and Yang,

Were well and truly trounced,

In the business of 'Search,'

By the Google gang,

It was Yahoo's board which bounced,

Microsoft's white knight hand[43],

Which was quite impossible to understand,

For all shareholders except Yang,

Who had clearly overplayed his hand.

Thus was a crown jewel,

Left worthless in the sand.

Blockbuster did Netflix spurn,

And in the streaming tide it overturned;

No guidance then on an approaching tsunami.

Enron's directors were more than willing,

To Lay themselves before Skilling[44],

Every tenet of governance going abegging!

Then, there's the story of NSE[45],

A Himalayan Swami did oversee,

Beyond the board's declared decree,

Which is both a blasphemy -

And a sorrowful irony.

---

[43] In 2008 Microsoft offered Yahoo US$ 45 Bn in a failed acquisition bid

[44] Kenneth Lay and Jeff Skilling were the Chairman and CEO of Enron, respectively. Its board was totally ineffective in unearthing their enormous financial crimes.

[45] National Stock Exchange (NSE) was rocked by a series of scandals which eventually led to the ouster of the CEO, Chitra Ramkrishna.

Directors – people of greatest eminence,

Most often picked for their allegiance,

Not for their fierce independence,

Ending up, to shareholders and CEO

Utterly beholden!

In a VUCA[46] world full of risks:

Keyman -- and succession

Scaling -- and digital transformation

Brand and -- ruined reputation

Credit, fraud and -- obsolescence,

Survive, not thrive the board's decree,

Skeptics' eyes, not friends they should be.

So often times these protagonists,

(Board and Management, that is)

Play roles of antagonists

With Machiavellian guile,

As dawned on Citi's CEO - a learned Pandit[47].

Despite performance splendid,

Was turfed by the board and asked to go.

---

[46] VUCA: World of business that is volatile, uncertain, complex and ambiguous.

[47] Pandit the CEO of Citi who helped put the house in order after the Financial Crisis of 2008 was summarily fired by the Chairman Michael O'Neill.

A successful board, to any great mind,
Makes a company anti-fragile,
Unshakable foundations it does forge,
Through a surreal balance,
Of support and challenge.
Powered by committees,
Of risk, audit, nomination
... And per chance even compensation!

Finding these trustees,
Often begins where it ends,
At the doorstep of luminaries,
Which an air of clubbiness portends.
The highest echelons of business,
Flag bearers of change and innovation,
Are themselves primed for disruption,
Untouched by tech or myriad inventions.

Posh part-time sinecures,
Or tough balancing acts:
Long-term vision,
With near-term traction,
Incentives and their fatal attraction,
Clawbacks' menacing retraction.
Rule-based; yet judgment laced!

Do boards need a new paradigm,

To offer something beyond the anodyne?

For the board's crown, truth be told,

Is not a hat that lets the rain in, oh no!

It's a beacon and fortress,

Against the winds that blow.

Survive, not thrive that's how it goes.

Your notes

STOCK EXCHANGE
09:15

Sonny's Money and IPOs

A 100-page IPO[48] prospectus distilled down to the essence by the key protagonists.

Roll call for the Cap table[49]

- *Founders (and Management) of the company*
- *Investment Bankers for the issue*
- *Exiting Private Investors – Angels, VCs, and PEs*
- *New Investors – Retail and Institutional*

Chorus: *(Raucous, champagne flutes held high)*

To hell with privacy, we're going public!

(Bank balances bulging; egos titanic.)

Founders: *(Eyes glazed with lucre's lure)*

Cash in your chips, folks,

It's like the oracle spoke!

We will do you all a solid,

And for the sake of liquidity

Accept your wired quid!

(Whispered aside)

Which'll our coffers fill;

Mansions, yachts and more still!

Investment

Bankers: *(Adjusting Hermes tie, scanning financials)*

---

[48] IPO – Initial Public Offering
[49] A table used to show ownership for a start-up or company.

There's a hole in the Balance Sheet,
Dear founder, dear founder!

Founders: *(With a cool air of entitlement)*
Then make it whole, my banker, dear banker!
Issue fresh equity for starters,
And the main course can come thereafter.

Exiting Private
Investors: *(Rubbing hands in glee)*
Not to forget our OFS[50]
And the promise of exit at 10X!

Investment
Bankers: *(Sharp suits, manicured looks)*
Scintillating story we will unfold,
For which adjusted EBITDA is pure gold!
Here's the list of anchor investors
And green light from the regulators.

Chorus: *(Energy and excitement writ large on faces)*
Everything around us grows multifold,
Apply for our IPO – for truth be told,

---

[50]   An IPO can also offer an exit for existing shareholders – this is an
OFS or Offer for Sale as opposed to new share issuance.

On the table we've left enough and more.

Join the frenzy, the dance, the golden glow,

In public markets valuations will fly even more!

New

Investors: *(Wide-eyed and eager. Clutching Offer Documents)*

Holy moly the future is here,

This unicorn's thoroughbred, my dear.

Management is exceptional, execution divine!

AI, ML and such things sublime,

Augur a bright future, to our mind.

We've gotta apply!

So, we feel no remorse,

At a future time!

Investment

Bankers: *(Triumphant smiles, sensing massive oversubscription)*

Passive, Active and Index Fund[51]

---

[51] Active Funds are managed by Fund Managers to beat an index. Passive and index funds on the other hand mirror an index and cost less to the investor. These were pioneered by John Bogle of Vanguard.

Are all lining up

For the forthcoming punt,

This stock is sure to sprint...

But do read the fine print!

New

Investors: *(Impatiently, waving aside all caution)*

The prospectus we've read,

By savvy investors we're led,

Isn't this the best thing since sliced bread?

Chorus: *(Champagne showers cascading)*

To hell with privacy, we're going public!

IPOs magic – wealth with liquidity!

The IPO is naturally a roaring success with the issue oversubscribed many times over.

Now it's listing day on the Exchange for the newly minted public company. The Founders, Investment Bankers, and Anchor Investors are beaming... (though not quite as much as the Exiting Investors):

They all await the opening,

At the Stock Exchange bell.

Qs: Does the stock list at?

a) Large premium to the issue price

b) Large discount to the issue price

c) Small premium to the issue price

d) Small discount to issue price

e) Around the issue price